*... I work harder to love myself, choose to
embrace my skin, flaws and all.
Every bump, every scar, I own it. Fun
being had. Smiling at myself.
Dancing to your songs, enjoying what is and what is to come,
fully knowing I can stand on my own ...*

Delaney Spellman has lived an abnormal existence. In her first collection of poems, she uses her voice to paint the fascinating picture she sees in her own life while encouraging others to never give up, even during the darkest of moments.

Within verse inspired from the depths of her overactive mind, Delaney intertwines illustrations with poems to form a compelling story of heartache, passion, and adventure as she explores emotions, invites others to see through a different lens, and provides hope to lost souls that they can realize a new beginning despite their obstacles.

The Truth That Hides is a volume of poems and original illustrations that reflects on a young woman's experiences while reminding anyone who is battling their own challenges that they are never alone.

THE
TRUTH
THAT
HIDES

DELANEY SPELLMAN

Archway Publishing books may be ordered
through booksellers or by contacting:

Archway Publishing
1663 Liberty Drive
Bloomington, IN 47403
www.archwaypublishing.com
1 (888) 242-5904

ISBN: 978-1-4808-8583-7 (sc)
ISBN: 978-1-4808-8582-0 (hc)
ISBN: 978-1-4808-8584-4 (e)

Library of Congress Control Number: 2019920171

Print information available on the last page.

Archway Publishing rev. date: 12/10/2019

For everyone in the darker times of life—
don't give up on yourself, and don't give in.

For the person I used to be.
Can you believe all that your pain came to be.
Thank you for fighting.

CONTENTS

FUTURE

To the body that lay lifeless on the bathroom floor but still inhaled, I see you. To the soul that was haunted by the lies others told, fight the voices that managed to dig inside of your head. To the one with dried blood caked on their thigh, it's okay to cry. Hidden behind locked doors, praying they don't find you, darling, push for your tomorrow. To the death that lived inside of me, know that you have no place in these bones. This is for the weak who bullied me every day. This is for the hopeless girl I was. This is for Satan, who attacked me every day. I now know my worth, and I have seen the future. I know where evil goes to rot.

ALL ALONG

Every once in a while, I stop to catch my breath. It's truly amazing the growth I have made since you left. I'd like to believe that you would be proud of me. As the days go by and leaves change, I start to recognize the change in me. It isn't so bad, not like I thought; maybe change is necessary for a person to develop. I want to say that you had a part in making me who I am, but I am different from you. I smile on command, and I can overcome the difficulties in front of me. I know you care, and you want the best for me. I am not the things that happened to me; I get to decide who I want to be. I'll love you forever. Don't get me wrong. Maybe the strength wasn't in you but in me all along.

SWEET DREAMS

I will never get a good night's sleep because while I lie
here in between sheets, I realize what's to come. Soon
you'll lie in the same position, 750 miles away. I'm crying
aloud inside my head. The stars, although I reach, are
still miles and miles from me. They may be bright, but
what comes next is day. So as I lie counting worries, never
sheep, I'll be reminded to cast my cares—not for a big part
but far away, just like you'll be, 750 miles from me.

HONESTY

Behind untold lies is proof how scared I am. You will no longer
be holding my hand. I know you have to be on your own; I
need to understand. Do what you need; I'll be okay. I'll say that
I love you through it all; the truth that hides is underlined and
signed. It reads that you're a part of me that will never leave.
Even in your absence, I'll stand in the mirror, reminding myself
you're still here on the lines of the truth that I underlined.

RENEWED

With lumps in my throat, I pray I don't choke. You can't see me this way. You don't deserve my pain. I smile all day and enjoy my time; that is, until I see my old friend. The moon cues the time and place where emotions come to scream in vain. I'm fine—truly nothing I can't handle. I'm not depressed, just stressed. Severely, I need a break, some time alone with the one who can conquer my demons; I want them no more. He is strong enough to erase this place. He will come to rescue me; not a knight but a king will come to save me. He loves me, and that's enough for me. My rope, he wants good for me, and I believe it's true. I'm not waiting to be saved; that's already done. I am waiting to be renewed.

THE GIRL I KNOW

There is a girl I know who gets anxiety when food runs low.
Those she knows try their best, but she gets pain in her chest
when she sees what's left. A girl I know hides when outside,
in fear that people from school will see where she is from.
The girl I know cries for help in her sleep because she feels
alone. Nightmares and empty bank accounts take over her
thoughts daily. But he will provide for her; he wipes her
tears and rids of the monsters that pound on her stomach
and in her chest. He casts out wickedness from her life. She
can't see him, but she should know even when she feels it,
she is never alone. My God provides for the girl I know.

NEVER FAILING

"Love never fails," means if it ends, it's not meant to be. Love is forever. If it all goes down and you feel the need to find a way out, trust, trust that it isn't love. When war comes around, trust that love will win. No one is against honest love. If you have to fight too hard, maybe this love is a security blanket. You deserve passion and something raw, and if it's right, you won't find yourself getting sick. Love never fails. This is true, so I remind you in hope that you will remind me it is worth it. We try so hard to obtain value from others. We don't need validation from someone else. Have we forgotten we have to be able to love ourselves? I don't want to lose you, so don't allow someone to destroy you. My wish for you is that eventually you will see how truly important you are. Is it worth it, forgetting who you are just so you can learn who someone else is? With your birth came value and importance. You are already significant.

DESTINED

You can handle what you face. If your back breaks, try using the hand of someone who will carry you home. When you can't find the right path, if you're scared, know that you're handed nothing that will destroy you; you decide if it cuts you. It's your choice. Cut the weight that will cause you to fall below; I will hold your hand. There is a way out. When you are left in the dark, seek the light. You will be granted sight. Break free, and finally, you will be who you are destined to be.

HARDEST TIME OF DAY

At the end of the day, when the makeup is removed and I am placed in front of you, when your glazed-over eyes pierce my soul, I know I will have to hear it because you're not as quiet as you were before. I will start to get sad when I notice the smile you once had has vanished, just like the hours of the day. As I stare at your face, I start to feel misplaced, as if we aren't one anymore. I see that you are trying your best to better yourself, but in some ways, you are still the same. I can't find the right words in order for me to say, "I forgive you." I forgive you for the years of abuse you have caused me. I forgive you for all of your mistakes. I want to forgive you for all of the damage you have caused. This wasn't supposed to be so hard, but it is. That is why standing here, in front of this mirror, is the hardest part of the day.

RESCUED

It's sad, but it's true; I am obsessed with everything you do.
Your beauty radiates off everything I love. I can't imagine
a day without; I am completely overwhelmed by the light
you shine. You warm my life. With cold hands and an active
thought, I know where I want to be—next to you every day,
passionate about what you're surrounded by. I enjoy the art
you create. I wrap myself in the thought of you. You are
everything to me. Like a wounded bird, I will care for the
things you hold dear. I will nurse the premature blossom that
will come. You have created a symphony inside of my soul.
You are my home. I have needed you for so long. I cannot
deny what you do to me. You continue to rescue me.

LEFT OR RIGHT

Thoughts of you continue to roam inside the head that stores my mind. The walls I have built keep me safe. Even though at times I wish the bricks would crumble, I trust that in time, you will come and march around me. You are the echo inside my head. I know that we aren't finished yet; too many things left unsaid. We weren't meant to be, but this is my next stop. Passing by and visiting at a later date—time is passing, and I don't want to sit around. Memories have to be made, good or bad. I would like to play this out, see what could have been. I want to experience life with you. I would like to look back and say there are no regrets. How will I know where I'm supposed to go if I have never lived, if I have never experienced the what-ifs I have created in my mind? Everything we do affects our lives, so I must decide—left or right?

SUFFOCATION

I can't breathe with you next to me, editing the words I have yet to say. There is no escape. I love you dearly, but you are always around me. I need space. I can't even open my arms. You have me wrapped too tightly, wrapped around your finger. The puppeteer, always together with no separation; you can say that I'm suffocating. It's not your fault. We weren't always like this; things have changed. There is no trust. You have forced me to revert to childish ways. I want what I can't have. Even with you wrapped around my neck, you are distant. Let's switch roles. I'll force you to do what I say and then disappear until you feel safe. You can call it toxic, and I will promise you it's because I love you and want to protect you. Don't you see? You aren't meant for me—not this time, anyway. I used to survive off you. You would exhale, and I would inhale. My oxygen was you, but lately, I find myself suffocating.

TALL FIELDS

The love I have for you is special. I didn't know that I was capable of hosting this emotion. More crisp than spring air, more vibrant than any of its colors, my love for you is sacred. My love for you waits until the timing is right. My love for you is never forced. This feeling is more than beautiful; it is the way I would hope my children to live. The promises it holds keeps me warm while gentle breezes flow across my face. My love for you has never been only self-regarding; I am reminded of all great things yet to come when you and I are together and apart. My love travels, desperately seeking out our next quest. With no fallback plan, we give it our all. I believe in us because you believe in me. Through tall fields and deep rivers, our love forever lingers. With everything we need, hand in hand we push through, never looking back, constantly moving forward.

MINE

Tell me how you felt when you first saw me. Did you instantly
know, or did it hit you weeks later, when you made me
smile? Are you confident in your decision, the way you are
confident in me? Every decision I have made has led up to this
moment. I fell in love with everything you represent. Always
striving to create something of a higher quality, your being
is admirable and personal. Electrical currents rush through
me when I see you. Your eyes shine and brighten up the
atmosphere. To be proud of something you didn't create is a
beautiful thing, To create something together is a blessing.

PULLED UNDER

I try to pry you out of my life. I try to walk away, but when you call my name, every flame you have created ignites in me. The passion you possess ties itself around my wrist; I can't pull away. I get strength to leave, but you pull me back. How could I leave when you have a grip on me. Back and forth, pacing the rooms and losing sleep, You and I on repeat. Underwater, you're the breath I need. If my head is above water, you're the chain wrapped around my ankle, pulling me under. We go in circles, burning for each other, slamming doors, and dramatic entrances. You're enchanting, and I am chained. But I won't complain.

COLOR

The fluff that blankets all that is above brings color to this life. I see what my childlike mind needs, shapes of combined pictures, pictures that swarm above my head, driving me to new places, following me every day. Why is it that today they really connect with me? Inspired by the way puffs dance for me, this is what clouds were made to be, never forgotten but appreciated for its effortless creation. They remind me to look for the message between, unwritten lines. They tell me of my better days and the tomorrow that is to come.

PICTURE IMPERFECT

Perfect pictures belong in frames, but important pictures are often stored away. Have you decided which you want to be? Most smiles come from perfect memories put away for a special time. We become immune to things we are exposed to. We see perfect pictures all the time, back to back. I enjoy the ones of your smiling face; those are the ones that make me feel a type of way. Our picture should be removed from the public, safe, something just for us. Broken picture frames are perfect for us.

BEST VERSION

Your eyes tell only the beginning. I look forward to exploring your mind. Tell me your nightmares, and we will plan our dreams. Quick on your toes, quick on my brain. How do you interact with those different from you? Your smile reminds me of someone I knew in a different life. I appreciate your personalities. Our inner children play well. Stay at least for a little while. I just want to know what you believe. What's your favorite scent? Why do I want to hold you like this? You make my stomach hurt from laughter. You raise these butterflies, made from scratch. I wanna know more. Show up just for the surprise. Never lie; your secrets will be my secrets. Embrace my independence. Be there for everything. Help me grow and be my best version.

HOUSEKEEPING

Your personality is sweet tea for the soul. Goose bumps
arise from me by the thought of you. You're arriving soon.
Housekeeping for the body, I'll tidy my surroundings to improve
your stay. Ready for new things; show me new experiences,
What's next, lazy days in, cuddled under covers, dancing in
the living room, karaoke in the kitchen, broken dishes, getting
through it together. I'm ready when you are, just waiting for
you to arrive. I threw out the dead roses and closed the photo
album. The box was removed from my closet; I think it's
in the Dumpster. I deleted a few folders stored in my mind.
Everything is clean now; I'm ready now. The clock has been
reset. Whenever you're ready, I left my baggage at the airport,
I don't want it back. I think you will like the new plants. I've
changed, and I'll continue to improve until you come through.

TAKE OUT NEEDED

I'll write it all down as a reminder. I'll reread everything sooner or later. What do you have to offer me? What will you do for me? How will you keep me? Never let me forget the nights you spent waiting for me. Will you appreciate how far I have come? Celebrate all I've become? Tell me your favorite things. Can't decide on my favorite quality. Consumed by your attention. Gentlemen, gentle man, your energy is all I need. You keep me hyped. I learned to trust you early on, safe with you. Wrapped in loving embrace, it doesn't hurt that I like your face. Tonight is one of those takeout nights.

BEAUTY

Learned how to command the room, in charge of my own point
of view. Embracing this season, confidence radiates. Don't need to
remain wrapped up in a phone. Care not about opinions. Thank
you, though. I work harder to love myself, choose to embrace my
skin, flaws and all. Every bump, every scar, I own it. Fun being
had. Smiling at myself. Dancing to your songs, enjoying what
is and what is to come, fully knowing I can stand on my own.
Independent but not selfish. Only a little stubborn, eyes opened.

VELMA

Flowering in the moment of time, watching as it unfolds before me, budding for their revival, seeds planted generations ago bear fruit for me to sow. They recognize hard work. I do it for those before me. It's how I thank those without me. Dedicated to the rose who has yet to bloom this year, we still acknowledge your beauty. The yearning soul, when I rest, I see you in my dreams. Forever young and forever here, I wish you were present, my perished primrose. May these memories never fade.

THE FLAME

I don't hate you. I do not want you. Even though I miss you,
I don't need you. I do not dream about you anymore ... any
more than four nights a week. I do, however, think about who
you said you were versus who you pretended to be. I could say
absolutely anything at this point, and it wouldn't matter; at,
all those times I waited. I don't love you. I do not hate what
we were. Even though we got burned, I miss the flame.

FORT

Build a fort, climb inside, hide away for the night. Sink into the cushions. Sink into a bliss covered by the covers and the shadow of the moon. Your eyes are our only light source. Doing what we do best, laughing at your stupid faces, our hands dancing together in this fort without an ounce of the outside world. It's nice to pretend that we don't have things to do. Tomorrow will come, but we can make this moment last. In our fort, our whispers are muffled; secrets stay in the fort. Popcorn scattered, old hoodies stained with your scent, I like being with you. Movie marathons and warm socks, memories to be made and words to be said. Our little getaway has made my day special. Our safe place will be remembered for years to come. Your company is always welcome. Our words on repeat in my head. The ache of a jaw is proof that with you, my smile never fades. Promise we can hide away in this fort every day.

BY YOUR SIDE

I promised to always be there, but what do you want me to do? You're never here, and it's cold this time of year. You can only add so many layers. My body was burning. It was only then I realized the cold was seeping from my internal being. You're preoccupied, living the dream I so desperately wanted to be a part of. Out of sight out of mind, right? We are drifting. It isn't you I hold close, but that bear you got me will do. Say you'll call, but when you do, I'm already sleeping; blame the time zone. Life is better together, remember? That's what you said before you kissed my head when you told me to be brave. I will stay because having to reschedule is better than never seeing your face after months of being away.

IT'S NEVER FAIR

I'm sorry. I know it isn't fair I keep running back to him. He would mess me up, and I called it love. You glued me together, and I would crawl my way back. You would find me and wipe the tears he caused. I would find myself in his twisted arms again. Again you would fix what he had broken. I lost you too. You couldn't understand why. I tried and lied to myself. Sure, he cared for me and four other girls. It was hard to watch you slip away. You went away, so when he pushed me down, you didn't throw me a life saver. I sank to the bottom to contemplate who was to blame. I cut the chain strapped to my ankle. He would've used me as live bait if I hadn't gotten away. I dug up my grave. I took what he stole. I washed my face; I took a stroll, My heart led me straight to you. I ripped open my heart to show you where I held you. You kept me safe. Your words led me to you. Can you see why I came? More than a friend, someone who knew how to save, I'm here for you. If you only knew outside your window once more. Not here for advice, I will cry on your shoulder one last time. I'll admit you make it easy to love myself. You make it easy to love you, and I do. That's why I kissed you.

YOU'RE GOOD FOR ME

The difference between a boy and a man is simple. He called me sexy; you call me beautiful. Respected every day and night, cherished and treated properly, you tuck me in every night over the phone. Never stay too late. Whisper encouragement, never hand-me-down sayings. Protect what's good in me. Proud, not intimidated. The man I prayed would be my future. Truly treasured, you inspire me always. You don't ask for a current location. A true man, you never put me in compromising situations. Invite to a special place. I don't need fancy things, just you. Remain true, that's what I admire about you. You read me every day, You are my favorite page. Ask me questions even when you know the answers just to hear me talk. Harmonizing for the fun of it, a natural connection. Love our connection, communication. I can't help but hope you're the one. You're good for me.

COMING

Something's coming. I feel it. Good things for me. I'm so excited, I can't wait. Sleep is a rare activity for me. I lie awake, staring at the ceiling, waiting. I know it's coming. Don't know when spring is coming. My winter will end.

EXPOSED

When water pours, it washes sores left from the days before.
Water cleanses my dreams; it removes tarnished hopes. I can
breathe when water rushes over me. Some may drown; they
have never been exposed to this element. I was meant to be
in this, consumed and amused. Pebbles run along the sides
of my feet, scrapping my bare feet. I will be washed away
and pushed through the drain. But not now, not today.

YOU

I know it's you. I saw you and knew. When I saw your eyes, it hit me. You are my future. Where you go, I'll go. I don't know how I am to get to you. The heart is loud. It tells all I need to know. It's you, looking forward to meeting all you are. I will learn your laugh, study your smile. I can't wait to hear your voice rise octaves when you explain the inside jokes, gagging on your laughter. I want to see you in a confused state. How will you react to my name? You are unaware, but it is clear to me: You, my love, are destiny. My eyes will take in your unkempt hair. When you wake up, what do you do? My heart can't wait to say your name. My soul is waiting for you. You don't know, so I must be slow. But my spirit screams that you're the one for me. Love at first sight is cliché. I must admit everything about this is insane. My head tells me this must not be; it doesn't make sense. Common or not, I will follow my heart. Our souls have already met. I guess I will wait and see, but I know that I know we will be face-to-face. You will see what is meant to be will be.

BEAR TRAP

Something so beautiful yet so toxic. Drawn to the shimmer, blinded by the artificial light. How did something so pretty morph into a shiny bear trap. You want to touch. But careful, they call her the mousetrap, snapped and bloodied. She wasn't always like this. They fly to her like moths. She's electric. Like an electric sting that never leaves, she won't leave them, not while they are in pain. She puts them out of their misery. It is not her fault she was caught in the trap of another. Does what she can to mute the static in her heart.

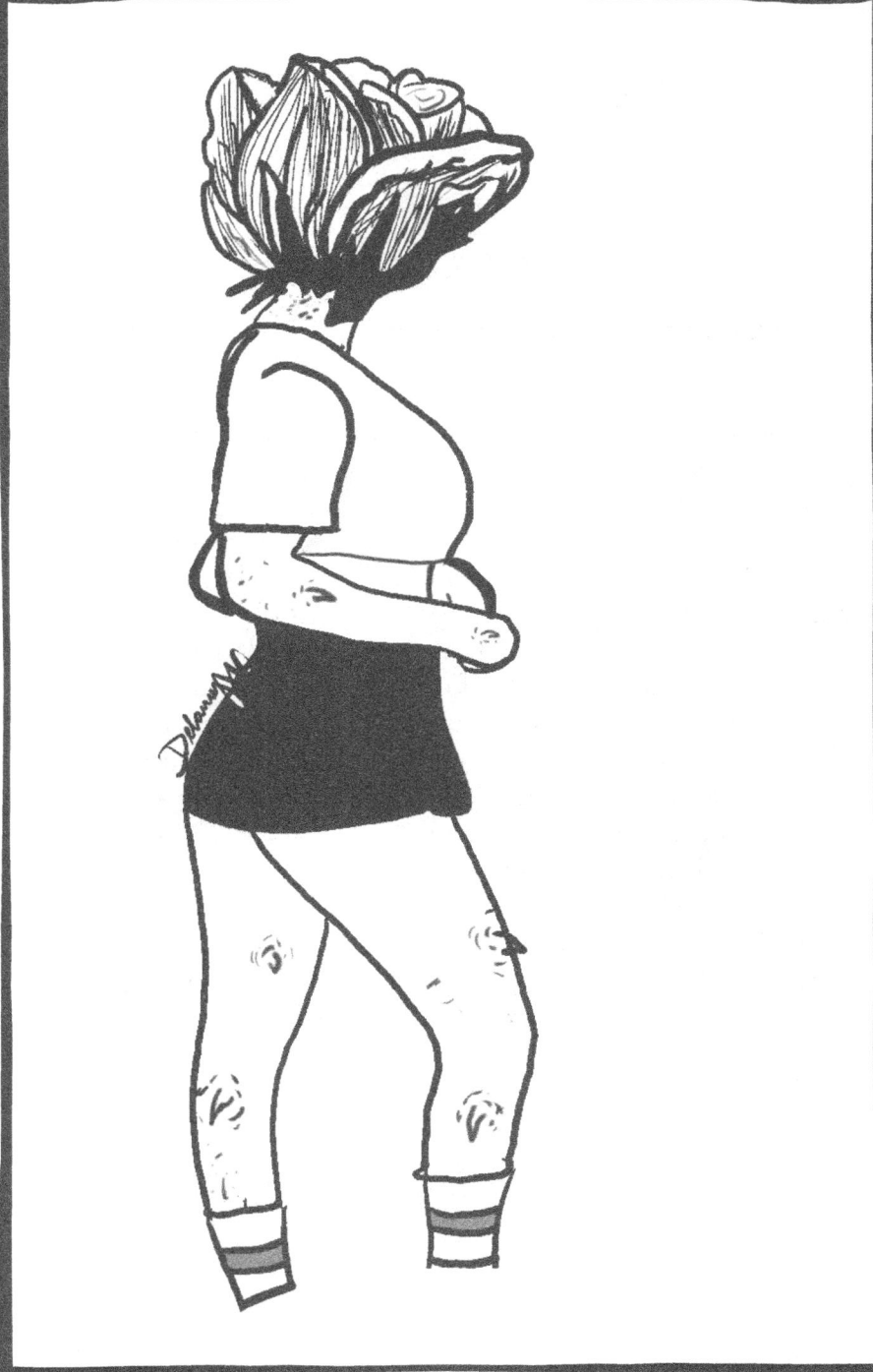

RECIPE

Trust is a vital part of any relationship. Without trust, there is no future. It's easy to obtain this trust, but once you break it, ashes. Ashes cannot be glued together. You can try, but everything will melt away, creating a mess. No one can clean a mess this big. You're spreading everywhere; it dries as cement. You have created something tormenting out of a beautiful thing. Four ounces of regret, one pound of betrayal, a dash of hard to swallow pills, and a pitched heart. Trust is the heartbeat of the relationship. I can't sleep because you're all I see. It isn't fair. Are you thinking of me? How come I'm the one suffering, Mix it all together. Add in the lies and tears from both sides. I miss you. I heard when you called it a mistake. A splash of lips. Note that for the recipe to work, lips must come from an outer source. You try to extract ingredients already added. How can I forget? Not rhetorical; someone tell me. I want to love him, but I'm hurting. See, we tried desperately to make trust, but you made betrayal. We can't have this; I can't serve this. Get yourself together, and we can make. I don't know if this will come out well. I'm not banking on it, but you can try.

ONE MORE

One more. I'm begging, please one more. Give me something to remember. I don't want to remember you like this. One more kiss before you go, When those doors close behind us, there will be no more. You will turn right and I left. There will be no more, we agreed. This is the responsible thing to do. When did you become responsible? One more hug; tears streaming down our faces. You breathe my hair in. Good things come to those who wait. Where are you going? Where am I headed? We don't know. I need to know. Will you give me one more memory? I don't know where to go from here because everything I once held dear is no more. To hear you say my name once more. Speak to me. Scream at me. Do anything, just please, I'm begging, give me one more. The sound of your voice continues to grow faint. I have gone on too long without you calling my name. You make it hard to go my own way. Turn around, please. Say something, please. Call me yours once more. I want to see your face light up when I enter the room. But now it is time to go. You no longer see me the way you did. These fences were meant to keep me safe. I thought you would be brave enough to climb it. You won't even try it. I said I was fine; I lied. You should know because you know me so well. You should know. Why, why won't you tell me why you let go? I don't know. Just give me one more. Wipe my tears once more. kiss me once more. spin me around once more. Do something, anything. Why aren't you listening? Once more please. Say you love me once more. Give me something to make this last encounter not so bitter. Please just say my name once more. I'd give anything to hear your voice once more.

ART

Art is so much more than shapes and color. Art is the beauty in the darkness. What we breathe. Art is movement of the body. We are art formed by God. Colors dance around me in perfect rhythm. We decide what is influential. Art is being moved by something so rare. Art is the words we speak, leaves in trees, a gentle breeze, your eyes looking at me, a baby's laugh echoing in a room. It makes us consider greater possibilities, like us. You are my favorite piece of art.

FREE FALLING

Curious, Who do you strive to impress? I want to free fall inside
your head. Just like you said, a field trip. I want to remember
your memories. I view you like a child observing the insect for
I do not know your purpose here. Is there a purpose for you?
My dear, If you were to read, what book would you pick up?
What kind of lines do you live by? I watch your patterns to see
what your next move will be. Would my grandmother approve
of you? Would she request that I leave you outside? I cannot
store you inside of the empty wet wipe container the way I did
worms when I was a babe. I must always respect Grandma even
though she has faded. What are your intentions, caterpillar?

CANDY

There are sores in my mouth. Sour candy has eroded the flesh inside of my mouth. It stings, but I continue to devour the very thing that's harming me. It's sugar-free, so it won't affect my shape. I'm told it's important to keep up with myself. It's too sour for my tongue, I have been cheeking it for protection, but it's doing more damage. I can't help it; I'm aware of what it's doing to me, but I can't break free. I break it down with my teeth, suckling on what lingers on the tip of my tongue. It's gone, but I have the scars to show. It will end eventually. You shouldn't touch fire to stay warm. I was cold, so I entertained myself with you. Sour, but I craved it. Candy isn't good for your health. It leaves you wanting what you shouldn't have. You fight with yourself because after, you are left with sores and an upset stomach. Why can't good things be more attractive? Why do you have to be so addictive? I'm going to pay for it. I can afford it.

CARBS

I miss carbs. They keep me warm. But I
am accepted now, so that's cool.

I SEE YOU

I had a dream of you last night. I sat beside you, comfortable, without worry. Everyone was around, I played with your hair. You welcomed touch; that's a good sign. Your friends liked my company. We all had fun, laughing at ridiculous remarks and banter. Your hand aligned in mine, I could hear the sound of your hair passing through my fingers. The way your lips hung when they made you smile. I could stay in this moment forever, but I would love to see our future. I listened to memories and created some of my own. Your T-shirt was marked with your scent, a scent that I wanted to store in a bottle forever, only opening it when you're not around. Smells can take you to a certain place and fill your mind with images of what was. When I smell you, I remember a life we had, a life I could have.

CHANGE

Change is here. Everything I know is changing. Which route should I go? Will I ever know which way is right? Will I fail, or will I fly? More than just words. In the end, everything I have done will pay off. I will be okay. Though nothing is the same, maybe new ways aren't so bad after all. Music calms the nerves in a crowd of others who are clueless as well. What if we are all winging it? What does that mean for you and me? Seasons new and old have prepared us for this. I have a lot to prove. Still, what will come of this? Will it be something others need, or is it what I need to be free? The whole point of this could really just be for me. I hope it will be a source of relief. Maybe I needed this to prove that I am good enough; I can contribute to the world. Words affect our souls, futures, loves. Words can change everything. I guess what I am desperately trying to say is I don't have to worry. What goes around comes around. I'm covered because I love him and have done things for him. What's to come is still unknown, but the best of me is yet to come.

KEN DOLL

He is great. My friends like him, and he works hard. Politeness consumes his personality. He enjoys my grandma and is constantly making others laugh. He's not hard to look at. Wants nothing more than to make me comfortable. He won't break my heart or lie to cover his poor actions. On the weekends, he wakes early to bring me coffee. He lives to make me happy, but I can't shake his flaws. All around he is perfect, but that one thing turns my stomach. With gentle hugs he makes my knees weak, weak with exhaustion. I can no longer keep it up because he is terrible. His jokes are lame, and my grandma loves everyone. And the way he strings his words together bores me. I don't even care for coffee, and he lacks excitement. My friends like him because they know he won't bring harm to a fragile heart. I need goose bumps from risky adventures. I need something he can't give me. I haven't cried in so long I am forgetting what a relief it brings. He won't allow me to feel any other emotion. I have to be happy with him, or he tries to fix me. He is cookie cutter, your average Ken doll, deserving of someone who appreciates his actions. It's unnatural for me. His face is always shaved, and he never challenges me; it's always my way. He will make someone very happy one day. I feel bad because at night, after he has left, I pull out your hoodie from the back of my closet and surround myself with heavy pillows. It's not my fault I can't sleep without your song. It's not his fault he's just not you.

DEEP

I'm in too deep. How can I go back? I don't know if I would
if I had the chance. Which path leads me to you? I will
gladly follow the directions sent from my heart straight to
you. In too deep, games are being played inside of my head.
The voices are loud, but if they lead me to you, I could get
used to it. The sound of your harmony, chords that heal.
Just imagine, I can't decide if I am being thrown or if I am
being levitated. I'm lifted higher, on another level, lodged
deep inside of my thoughts. So much to decide and to
determine. Still too young to have everything planned.

PURPOSE

I think we are all searching for our purposes. We want to understand why things are the way they are, waiting every day, trying to complete this impossible task. Maybe that's part of it. If we knew why things were, we would still be united as people. We know what has happened, but do we truly know who is to blame? What factor switched everything around? We can't go back and change. Does this mean we would hold grudges? I guess it's not that important. Who's to blame? Perhaps the best thing is choosing to move forward. They say anything is possible. I trust in what God says; He makes all things possible. If it is His will, I will soar, deciding along the way which steps to take. I want to do it all. I will write, I will sing, dance, and paint. I will find any reason to celebrate. I want big things. I dream boldly. Who says I have to have limits? No one puts restriction on those of success. Who says I won't get there? I don't need others to support it. It would be nice, but I can do whatever I set my mind to. If I use all of my might and keep my prayers constant, I will be what I choose to be. God, be with me.

PERSONAL

I don't know if I will attach my name to these words. I don't know if I can admit these are my thoughts. If I claim what is upon these pages, I will have to face the truth. These words have me so exposed, wounds and expressions open for judgment. I can't help but fear the judgment that will follow raw feelings. You shouldn't be reading something so personal. Honesty tells me to own what I think, but these thoughts won't let me sleep. What parts are still just for me? No one knows what really goes on in my brain. Who says this isn't already filtered? If I say that I wrote this, it means I can't hide. My thoughts are here. Paper has never scared me the way it does now. I would prefer this book to be left on the shelf, collecting dust along with those other books you promised you would read. I don't tell my closest what rattles in my brain, but I allow others to view it. I confuse myself. Please put it down. It's too important for you to drop it. You will put it down and move on eventually, but what about me? What do I do? An open book or a personal diary I have yet to decide.

BEFORE

You didn't say it, but I can see it: I have upset you. I tried to brush it off, but I couldn't. It consumed me, so I started speaking to myself. I had to wash it away. I got in the shower to wash it off. I scrubbed away skin cells, watched them circle the drain. Sensation burning. I scrubbed myself raw and numb. I can see how I ruined your mood, bothersome and unwanted, insecure because I never meant harm. I can feel it. You're irritated. I'm sorry, I irritate myself too. I wanted to sink down into the floor. I didn't, worried you wouldn't believe in me. Exaggerating. The pain isn't heartburn. Anxiety wrapping me in self-doubt. You moved on; I'm paralyzed. Where did I go wrong? How can I fix it? It's the small things that make you tick. I should have known better. Be honest, is it me or you? Were you happier before? My insecurities tell me it's me. Were you always like this? Tell me. I can't be blamed when I'm not around.

SURVIVE

I'm done. I can't be your only source of happiness. I can't stay. I am the one you blame when it rains. I have decided to care for myself. You taught me that I was selfish once I started thinking about myself. Who will look after me? I am too busy walking on eggshells to be walking in a decent direction for myself. I'll do what you want, but I can only jump so high. I want to be your definition of selfish. I want to care about and cherish my mental health. I'm not kicking you out, but the door is open. I have yet to consider my options. Do I trust no one? Is it a sad way to live or the only way to live? Do what you want, but expect me to do the same? It's not about you anymore. I'm not double-checking with you anymore. You complain when I grow. You get aggravated when I'm dependent. I'm no longer pretending to be disabled. I'm running to what I need. What do I want? It is such an odd thing to consider my feelings. Never even stopped to calculate the damage that has been done. I needed you then and would like you now. I stand on my two feet. I climb solo.

I have to be selfish during this time. I'm trying to survive.

OPPORTUNITIES

Empty places filled with blank spaces. Opportunities, things
that could be, Chances that will create me. Climbing out of
the shell that housed me, I want to risk it all just to see. I study
everything in front of me, breaking cloth that contained my
being. Seeking new possibilities. Courage taking over, pushing
through even when it seems impossible. Moving forward,
compressing the fear, I don't care to be realistic anymore. I crave
a deeper understanding of what's around me. Slowly removing
the weeds in my path, the sky is clear from here. My path is
clear up here. I'm proud of who I gained. Not always fearless,
I am courageous, chasing the developing dream. I won't let
anything limit me. I can see what was blinding me. I can. Pushing
through, I will see the truth. Everything I once knew has been
rewritten. I'm not prepared, but I will learn along the way.

TO ME

You think I'm in control. You have no idea the effect you have on me. Happiness stems from your beautiful soul. I promise never to harm you. You have all of the ammo you need, however, you would never hurt me. To me, you are the difference between night and day. To me, you are the summer rain, sun after a series of dark days. To me, you are shelter. To me, you are kind to me. I'm waiting for the right moment to spoil you. I want to thank you for your support. I appreciate your hard work. You're the light I need.

PURITY

How can I keep it down, the contents of what energizes
me. Nutrients that strengthen me. How come what's good
for me makes me feel unworthy. Not another bite; must
fit into the mold created for those like me to be wanted,
to be loved. Maybe our perceptions of beauty are the
toxic things, more than skin deep. Perhaps I'm not the
ugly one. Your mind has lied to your swollen heart.

FADE

It's not about lust or desire. I don't need what the world is feeding me. I need someone who can keep up with me; I am worth the wait. I will never beg. Cherish me or leave, I will be okay, standing firm in who I am. I don't have to tell you because you and I are the same, hoping to be enough.

You explain that it's me. This is ours. Forever has never seemed so short. You make me feel some type of way. Pure is expensive; it can't be tainted. We will never fade.

UNSURE

I'm unsure. Did I waste the days of my youth? When age comes for me, will I think fondly of my upbringing? What could've been runs through the thoughts trapped in my head. Coldness surrounds brittle bones. Will the future be enough to warm my foundation?

CROWD

I don't have the energy to pretend that we will be okay. You exhaust me. I don't want to be social. I would rather be home. I just want my bed. I don't belong here, not with you, not with them. Thought it was a good idea. When did I start listening to myself? I'm just trying to leave; I don't belong here. Can't believe I bought an outfit for this. I could be watching reruns or reading my new book. I planned for this event, but I didn't plan an excuse. I would leave if their attention wasn't on me. I can't fake it. I hate pictures. Just take it. I'm uncomfortable; it wasn't worth the wait. Someone transport me out of here. The windows in the bathroom are too high. The music out there is too loud. Lights don't have to be that bright. I should've cancelled. Maybe if I fake diarrhea. Maybe too far but an appropriate description for this night. "Y'all go ahead," I'll order, just to clear my head. I don't belong in this crowd.

OUR WAY

At one point you will look up and realize everything is right.
Every tear cried has landed you here, exactly where you're
supposed to be, your daydream brought to life. This is where
we are supposed to be. We didn't realize all of the memories
made. This is the time I created in my head. This is where
God has planted me, This is what He had in store for me,
peace washing over me like a warm summer breeze. Beauty is
a destination, not a location, Beauty is created by smiles and
laughter. Nothing in life is ever perfect except this moment. I
woke up and realized who is in control. Freed, decisions of my
own, laughter echoes and rattles inside of my soul. The rise
and fall of a chest alive and thriving. Water coursing through
veins. We got this, whatever comes my way, our way.

HEARTBEATS

I held on so tightly my fingers bled, knuckles purpled and stained red, white and pale. Sometimes holding on does more harm than letting go. A thorn piercing a throbbing heart drained of energy and emotion. High off fumes that emerged from the ashes, they all fall down into muggy waters. They can't breathe. Tears flow from faces like splattered paint on a splintered canvas. Clothing ripped, mauled by lies. If I survive, don't call me alive. Stripped of pride, I choke on blocks of complication. I would take a rusted axe to the arm over your double-bladed tongue to the side of my brain. I wish for my mind to rot; I hope that it would prevent me from thinking of you. Even a bruised heart continues to beat for none other than you.

NUMB

Is she the answer to your prayers? Is she the one I couldn't be?
I try so hard to sleep, but you own my dreams. I can't swallow
the truth; you are the lump in my throat. Is she who you dreamt
of? Is she who you have been longing for, waited for? Tell me
the truth. Is it because of the view? I tried to be happy for you. I
want only the best for you. I know these words curse, but I see
right through. She's not the one for you, not out of jealousy but
out of love. If I'm no longer the one you need, then understand
I can still read you. I know your thoughts. You are trying to
heal, but she will only infect our wounds. If you're trying to
move on, do what you must, but trust me. I know you're trying.
I know your pattern. You will get hurt just to get numb.

LOVED BY YOU

I see what you're doing. You are giving them the strength to carry on. Come nightfall, there will be a change. You love us. You protect us from what is on the outside. You're the guide for all who are broken and to all who are stable. You have always been there. I will sing a new song. It's not about what I went through, it's about who you are. Why haven't I been able to see this? Was I really this blind from the darkness? It's always been there; I just had to open my eyes. You're magnificent and glorious and justifiably so. You mend the broken, and you rob the grave. You are the author. Such a brilliant creative mind, All beauty came from you, from your hands. He is the painter of the sky, the ultimate of everything. He is the I Am, and you are loved by him.

STAR

The inspiration that comes from the star is intangible. I saw it flicker among the rest. I tried but couldn't feel the hurt. It was like I heard some stars die. They struggle to compete, afraid of never being bright enough, worthy enough, deserving of an admiring eye. Moved, I couldn't ignore the one that stood out, fighting to maintain the light left inside. My gaze shifted across the sky, locking focus on a familiar shutter. Though they felt alone, there was indeed another. The light was weak for this star has let others borrow from it. Caring for others was the nature of a small fading star. Desperate to give others a chance, it gave until weak but never drew attention. The light will eventually fade, and its acts will soon be forgotten. Struggling in silence, the star grew frail after accepting its fate, giving up what was left to ensure survival of the other. Our original star grew bolder with its borrowed light, shining brighter than the rest. Others rejoiced the recovery. The last breath was exhaled as the weak light softly fell after giving its all. The sky was silent, and a breeze came swiftly to mourn the lost. The night continued.

RECORDINGS

I fell asleep to your voice last night. I shouldn't depend on you like this. I prepared myself to be a lot stronger than this. Then you come and demolish her everything. I shouldn't need you, but I'm happy with you. I thought I was stronger than this. I miss you. Shouldn't need you. I listen to an old recording because it keeps me company. You're not here, and it's taking a toll on me. How did I let myself become so fragile? I guess it's your special ability, For years I tried to be independent and worthy of self-love, and then you came and wrecked everything. I allowed you to remold my heart. You carved your name inside, called me yours. I would do it all over again just to see you. It's been a while. You said you could come back, but until then, I will cuddle myself while listening to old recordings of back when.

FACE IT

I've been waiting for you, praying that there would come a day
when you would wake up to say all that you have been dying
to tell me. The words you so desperately want to spew from the
depths of your mind flowing to the tip of your tongue, dancing
behind your teeth for acceptance. Don't hold back. I want to
hear what screams behind those soft eyes, to be filled with your
words. My ears would love to hear your stories. Don't be afraid
to share with me, Intimidated by my stance, fill my head with
the words you think. Don't be afraid. Just tell me. Face it.

PINTS

I became a stereotype today. I bought a pint of ice cream to get over you. But once again, I made another mistake. I got dairy-free. It's disgusting, But it matched my mood, so I shoveled another spoon. I guess dairy-free doesn't work because it's still sitting in front of me, melting as I write about you. One more bite, I swear. It smells gross, similar to my stained T-shirt. I went to paint, but it felt like a task. So I sat on the cold floor, continuously shifting to accommodate my boney butt. It expires in three years. Even this pint lasted longer. I didn't know who to feel sorry for, me or the dairy-free beings. I've had enough, not of this ice cream but of these feelings. It's actually grainy, reminding me of the night we escaped to the roof. Barefoot, we held each other close, wishing for greater to come. I'm not feeling well. Stomach is hurting. Without a doubt, I know it's from the broken heart oozing into the empty pit, but I'll blame the coconut milk.

FLASHBACKS

I rediscovered my favorite picture of us while cleaning my closet. I spent the rest of the night strung out on the floor. I saw you cross over to the other side once you saw me. I was at your favorite place, hoping to run into you. I kept my head low and took it to go. I didn't want to let it go. Don't let me become someone you used to know. If you see me, please remind me with your speech. Wave or force a smile. Don't allow bitterness to define us. Does your head not remember what my heart cannot forget. Your love still pumps in my veins. I'm begging to hear you say my name. Why would you turn around at the sight of my face? What happened to never being replaced? I know you still care about me. You have useless facts stored in your brain, and your fingers memorized my number. How can you keep walking? It is too soon. Healing isn't an option. I'm too tired to continue on, looking forward to just staring at my ceiling. I can't close my eyes because flashbacks are on replay. It stings to blink. What will happen tomorrow? Will you ever forget my middle name?

LIES

I know I did the right things, so why is my skin burning from the cold weather. I couldn't hold you back, to release you when you would rather sink. Just like our dreams. What if I can't find another one? No one compares. I pushed you out because you needed to fly. I can't go where you are going. I lost something so irreplaceable so that you would gain the world. I promised to never tell. You couldn't handle being responsible for all of this. You would've thrown it all away if it meant my happiness. You're selfless. It wasn't the lack of emotion that ended us. I put you first. You would kill me if you knew I caused a scene just to protect your dream. Go and make a change. I will never be able to give you that world. Years from now, after you have accomplished the world and have seen big things, if you haven't met someone new, trust that my heart still houses you. How could I release the grip on my everything? I want nothing more than to call your phone. I need you to come over. I need you to live to the fullest. I kicked you out. I'm sorry, but you had to think I was over it. I refuse to hold you back. I'm secretly wishing you'll come back home to me. I will forever support you. You said you would stay, but we both needed you to go.

CLIMBING OUT

When a house is not a home, when relatives are not a family, when left to figure it all out by yourself, pray for a future. When you want to fall apart but you know no one will be there to pick you up, daydream. The life you're living doesn't have to be the life in front of you. Refuse to lie down. Picture life years from now. If it doesn't flip your stomach, flip it around. Demand better. Survive for yourself. Think of yourself. Who will chase your dreams if you sit on the bleachers? I want to break out. My only weapons being my two hands, I'm breaking windows. He's breaking down walls that held me captive. I'm scared and covered in scabs from head to toe. Absolutely covered and bloodied. But I'm out, and I'm making changes.

CONFIDENT

I know you're not trying to tell me how to be. I'll wear what I
want; I'll do what I want. My perfection doesn't come from a
tube. I believe that I can do what makes me feel confident as
long as it follows my rules. I would never belittle or gossip about
their decisions. Worry only about me. Selfless but conscious of
what's best for me. Humble and confident to be comfortable
enough to block out their comments. When I look in the mirror,
I want or see me, lines by my eyes, freckles on my cheeks.
Imperfections make me human, Why would I hide that? Bags
under my eyes tell a story of staying up late just to hear your
voice on the other line. Our bodies are scrapbooks lined with
bumps and scarred flesh. I'm all for it. Used to be terrified of
showing a bare face, but a natural flow can't be replaced.

FABRIC

Why do we form opinions based on the fabric others drape their bodies with; we have clothing define our styles. Many styles, but aren't they all the same? Colors fade, and threads stain. If we're able to remove the cloth in pure innocence, would we be able to see past it all? Our design, different colors, and different shades, shapes, all sizes. Is there truly an ideal body? Your starting point is someone's goal. We let this all get out of hand. His jacket is big, and his pants are littered with pockets and zippers. Her shorts are too short with a top that doesn't do her justice. Determined to be me, I'm not your average. I find myself to be well rounded. Nice blouse with dirt on the jeans. At the end of the day, material is all the same. I can't even remember what I wore yesterday.

LENSES

I have yet to find a way to express what rattles in this mind. It can be confusing at times, trying to decode emotions and feelings. Everything known has shifted. Tilted images, I have to adjust the lenses.

STINGS

I try to find my identity, but the trash surrounding me buries deep, becoming my gravity, defining me. Written on these walls are my silent screams; hopes and dreams smashed against rotting plaster. Forced grins slammed on my face. All emotion must be pinned back. I have let them ruin me. They never leave. Following me, I can't escape the life they've created for me. I scrub to get clean, but it still clings to me. Their words, their habits. I hide behind closed doors because I know they don't open for people like me. My skin stings. I long to be different from those around me. I have decided to create the true me.

HOME BASE

I don't want to wake up sometimes. I stay up late thinking about who I used to be. That little girl was so brave, Broken but courageous. Then my mind drifts to you. I was so wrapped up I didn't care that you wrecked me. Life has altered itself drastically since we parted. They say things happen for a reason. What was our reasoning? I came out stronger, mentally, We couldn't last forever, but I wouldn't change a thing. We taught each other patience and gave ourselves hope. A life, although not together, is full of possibilities. We understood what would come, but we never talked about me leaving and you moving on. I miss your present soul that brightened troubled days. We have so many private jokes and inside sayings. Memories that can't be tainted. Perfect timing, wrong season. If only factors weren't the same. If clocks could freeze. You were mine for a while. Bittersweet history. I think of you often. I know you are doing well. Whenever you're feeling misplaced, you ask to see my face. I know that all is going okay because my phone doesn't ring. I'm here for you always because you were my safe place.

ENOUGH

How do I protect you from your own decisions? How do I tell you have changed, and I can't be around you? I can't stand who you have allowed him to make you become? I blamed him for so long. I must see. You have made up *your* mind. Goodbye.

LAST GOOD THING

You should be here. Words so thick teeth shift when I speak. A pressure that makes me weak. I can pretend you're next to me, but it will never protect me on the darkest night. The moon comes to remind me of your travels. Where you go I will never reach. You should be here with whom you claim to love. What shall I look forward to? The sun will rise and shine right through my transparent eyes, glazed over, waiting for your return. How could you? I don't blame you. We all want to leave. You were the only thing holding me in this town. My ties are released, but if I leave, will I ever be found. When you come looking, I want you to hear of the things I've done. You were the last good thing in this town.

LEAD

I want to be inspired. I want to be honest and thrilling. I want words that I speak to touch hardened souls. Crippled by jumbled letters, stuttering over my purpose, can I do this, lead others?

FORGET

I don't want to think about you anymore. I don't want you to
have control or power. Not anymore. I can't bear the thought
of your touch. I can't allow myself to remember the sound
of your voice when you called me yours. I won't let myself
relive the days of us. I want to shut it out, put it in a box with
a broken lock so I can revisit when I'm isolated. No one can
know that you still take residence in my thoughts. I need to give
you up. I want one last hug. I must move on and forget you.

GRIEF

You're not here. Where are you? You said you would be here when I needed. Where are you? I have checked every spot of ours, every hideout of yours. Everything is fading from my graying hands. Where are you? Not in my embrace or my place. I search until my eyes cloud with the sea saltwater you supply. I can't, not anymore. My feet are tired, my knees bruised. I can only crawl through so much broken glass. The shadows of the past are all that surround ~~us~~ me. Where are you? Bleeding hearts and pleading souls, empty rooms and vacant sheets. You said you were tired. Where are you?

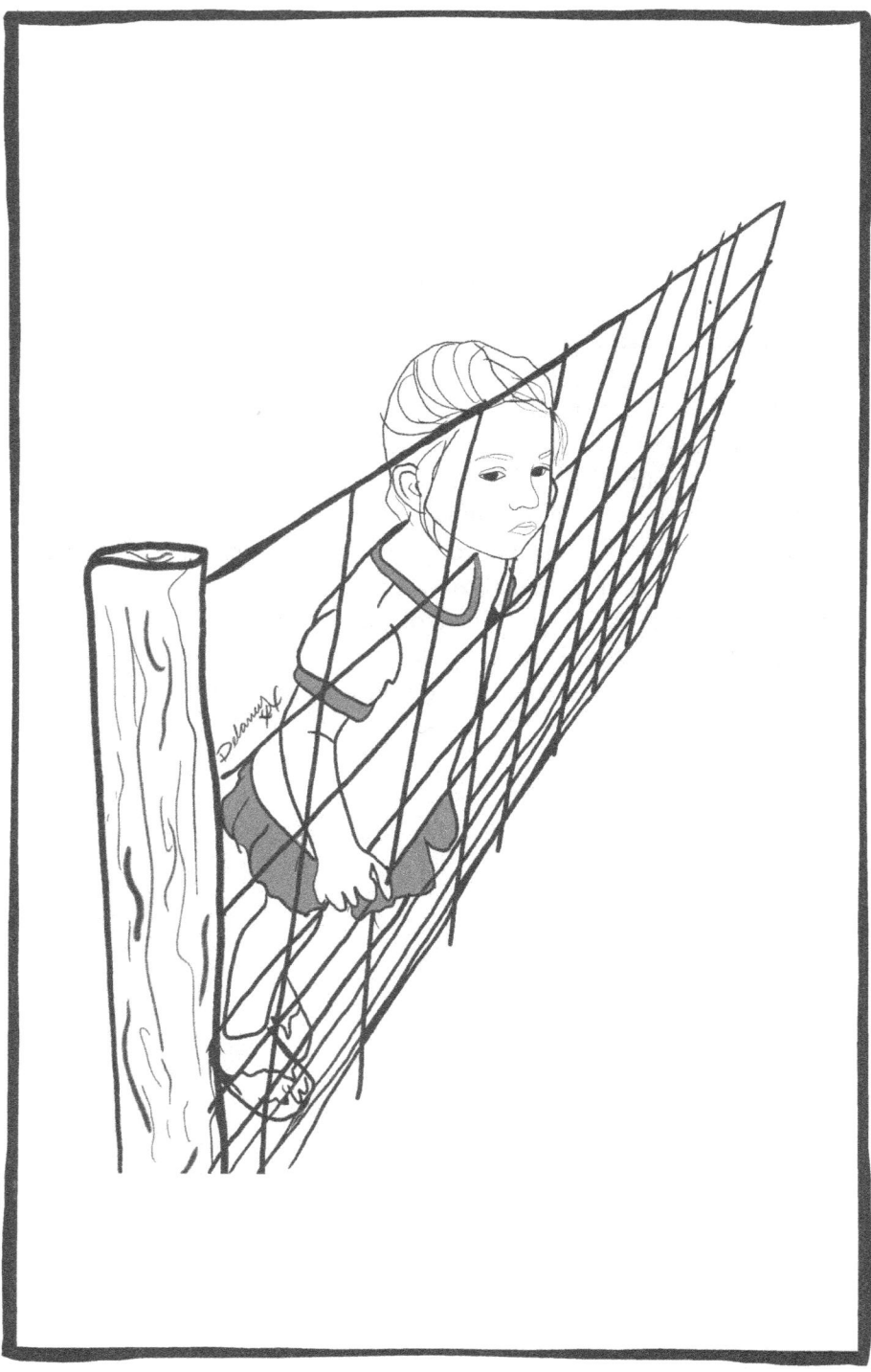

FLESH

Nervous about picking the right words, what do I say to make them believe I'm sane? Have they failed to realize that I am, in fact, human with emotions that change often? I don't want to admit that I'm vulnerable. I am not like them because of whom I follow. However, I am still flesh and bone. I am not the same.

HOLLOW

What will I do? I forgot to bring headphones, so I'm stuck. I shouldn't be annoyed so easily. The lack of common sense, my lack of compassion, I won't be able to adjust them, but I might be able to fix a calloused heart. I have seen much, which has made me cold. I stopped listening to the birds years ago. The guilt I feel gives me relief. The same girl is here, but she is knocked out cold in the corner. I have to wake her before the butterflies lose their color, before I lose my sense of humor. Was it I who let myself fade away? There is no one left to blame; I pushed them away. The sound is much too loud for me. They are quiet, but the sound is inside of me, bothering me. Hard to breathe. Can't believe I let myself slip into this state of pondering. I have spent the night chasing hollow thoughts in my head. Wasted too much time in this bed. Everything relates to another. Blurred behind tired eyes, and I can't hide what I want to keep safe. If I keep it to myself, I can protect the little girl who has yet to see the world.

YESTERDAY

Smile and vehemence. They tried to shush us up, but we couldn't contain the laughter. All out on the table, snorting and trying our best not to pee as mess. I'm okay if we never mature, pure friendship drenched in comical relief. Never forget days like these. We have to be bothering someone, interrupting their quiet time. We try to be polite; It doesn't work when you look at me with that ridiculous smile. We might actually get kicked out if we can't behave. Who says you can't have fun when it rains? Who told you there was a time limit with healing? We make our problems melt away, willing to forget the pain that came with yesterday.

DAGGERS

Words like daggers around my throat. I know this time I'll choke. Bound to trip and miss my step, face-first. I give it all I got with little in return. I find it hard to tell you the truth. I've never been much of a liar, but I have never stayed quiet either. Wasted ink and energy. Nothing left remains. Why are you so hard to forget? Even on the days that I claim as mine, you are there in the breeze that kisses my cheeks. My love spills over and drowns the fish I once loved. I have never been this open. I don't let people in; I have found that they track in mud. You say that your shoes are clean, but I'm too scared to check. I don't like liars.

SNIPPED

I can't pretend that you weren't a part of my life. What I thought was friendship you considered an opportunity. I can't even call it a beautiful tragedy. I just need to know my next step. I didn't listen because I've heard your words before. They were gentle but aggressive, easy to drown out. Now I'm here with split veins that cry out your name. Withdraw. Can't sleep. Everything I had left me when I chose you. Everything I chose failed me when power was abused. Keep moving. They say take the next step. Feet made of lead, Took what you wanted and fled. Used for what was left in me. Sometimes I wish I couldn't see. I was told evil has the prettiest face. This was truly disgrace. Chosen family shouldn't have been so selfish, jealous, obsessive. Control was all you had to your name, searching for your puppet on a string, commanding my every move. Owned by you, jerking me around, the goal to break me. Stripped of my pride, slipped into the dark. Abused by your love, chords wrapped around my throat. Fought for my life. Free from your claw. Snipped.

SUBTLE

You can tell me that you love me, but that doesn't mean you do. Subtle action is how I know the truth. I can see the train, and I don't want to move. Do you? We can't stop until we crash. We are both passengers. Who knows who is driving? All I know is that this burns. I guess that's what flames do. We are waiting for the flames to engulf us, take no prisoners. This is who we have become. I have tried to collect the dust, but it slips through my fingers like fragments of glass. Destined to be broken, we aren't meant to last forever. I appreciated the care given. Nothing left but remains of coal. Is this really how we unfold? They continue to keep their eyes closed. Couldn't take it anymore. Could you? Heat of the moment or relief of the pressure, I haven't felt wanted for quite some time now. Can only apologize so many times. Now it's just insulting. The night is over, but what are we? Do we go forward, or do I allow you to take a part of me? Sincerely yours. Or was.

ME

How dare you make ignorant judgment on my flesh. Why am I so offended by your blunt words? Who knew this is what I'd feel, used and exposed? Why would they set me up only to fall like a porcelain doll slipping off its rod. I thought I would be salvaged from this dirt. Probably not good for you right now. I fell asleep waiting to be saved from the roots that ground me, leaving me stuck in this old rut. The dirt was kicked in. I can't wait for you to settle on your present. I'm stumbling now. You can't be bothered by fixer-uppers. That's fine. Just know you can't change your mind when I chase down success and make myself a name. I fight for what I have faith in Me.

FOOT MOVEMENT

Why don't more people dance? Have they forgotten
the freedom provided by movement? I dance behind
glass doors, doors covered by thick sheets. I try to be
transparent, but I prefer frosted windows and clouded
glass. If they see my movement, they could use it against
me. My signature is something I use to make statements my
mouth can't say, things I'm not yet ready to deal with.

UNIQUE

I tried to be like the others, but I'm not used to it. I can walk it, but I can't pretend to be anything other than me. I like me. I'll stick to being unique.

GONE

When it gets difficult, I will hold you through it all. When you fall with no one to catch you, I'll support your landing. I can't prevent you from running back to the one who kills your aspirations and dreams. It is only I who sees what the beast hides. Your potential will never be reached when you continue to chain yourself to a thief convicted of stealing the person I used to know. I miss you, who you used to represent. I haven't seen joy in your eyes in quite some time, Why is it like this? I won't blame you, but if you would have listened, just maybe. I can't save you; I never had that ability. So tell me who is the lost one? I lost you, but you lost yourself. Torn between leaving you and needing to fix you.

BACKBONES

I needed this break because I had to figure out exactly everything
I wanted in my life. In this time, I have realized I depend on you
way too much. I want nothing less than all that you supply. I
crave your presence throughout the day and during the night. You
go out of your way in relentless pursuit of my happiness. I trust
that you were made for me. You have given up everything. You
satisfy any and all of my needs. That is why I have to let you go.
When a backbone becomes something I don't own, I must protect
the one who possesses it all. I could never manage being the one
who disables a generous man. Please allow me to work on my
independence. Don't feel the need to wait, Continue to live your
life, and if we meet on a higher level, maybe we could let this be.
However, in this time, I must rediscover all I am supposed to be.

CHARITY

I will never be a charity case, one in need of a prince. It will be on my feet in which I stand to fight my own battles. I have promised that I wouldn't grow with someone unless I could prove myself not to be a weed. I'm not one to be clingy, and I don't need someone to come mend me. Through Him, I will fix unforgiving flaws. I will flip the moon around and tear down walls or climb them. I will meet you on mutual ground. If I'm not stable, why would I allow a love to try and heal me? I'm looking for fifty, equal parts. I will be fair. You won't have to reassure me because I will find the beauty in myself first.

ONE-WAY TICKET

I need a one-way ticket Any other place than here. I need a
one-way ticket to get me outta here. More than a vacation. It
gets hellish in the dark. I close my eyes to try to find a nicer
place to rest my head at night. I don't need rainbows, just
plants and sunshine to burn away the mold stuck to my past.
I need a one-way ticket that can pull me out of these bricks.
Weight lifted from my chest relieves the blood pounding in
my wrist. Sunburns welcome sleep I haven't had in weeks, a
drowsiness I find relaxing, the smell that comes with chasing
winds. I need a ticket. I want to create a vacation place I can
call home. Boards and nails build shelter, but what will build
me a home? I have seen great things and new ways, dreaming
of the waters while longing for a fresh beginning. For me, I
need time and a new place. I bought a one-way ticket. I won't
come back; I crossed my heart. Only I know the location
of my destination. A little secret, my one-way ticket.

BATTERED

Muffling the noise, zoning in and out, can't concentrate on the task at hand. Never thought my demand would show itself this strong. The brain is a funny thing. It never shuts down. Even after I have shut it down, it blinks, flashing memories and what could be. It never shuts up, no matter how high I scream. All the deals I have made slip through battered screens, reminding me that I don't have to hide. If I decide on a life like this, I'll never be found. Swallowed coughs and achy eyes plan on stealing the little that is mine. Mine. Little things I hide, trusting that no one will come close enough to see what is really bothering me. You didn't fight to say goodbye. You packed and left. Left me to wonder if I forced you away. I try not to do things in vain, which is why I vanish. I want to, I want to try, but the muscles in my body are too weak to be seen, let alone to be used. When my pen runs out of paper, you can go on. But what about me?

Thoughts that bleed. No amount of pressure will cure this pounding mind. I wouldn't mind if the voices just whisper, but it is never just a whisper. I am in desperate need of a peaceful sleep. Be removed from my eyes if not from my mind.

MIDDLE

I don't have time to wait for all of these problems to subside. I reach forward, trying to fast-forward all of the hardships that come along. I don't want to wait; I want the happy ending. But I don't want anything handed to me. They say what matters most is what's in the middle, but how will I know when I am in the middle? Since I haven't a clue where I'll end up, I guess I can live for the moment. I dream of open clouds and endless possibilities. Dreams that come true are never handed to you. It's true. I'll bust my rump and put myself into overdrive, striving to make the life I want to live.

COUNTING

You apologize because guilt consumes. Now, what am I supposed to do? You find alleviation in confiding in me, but where do I go when your hurt trickles on to me? You're hurting, and I can't help without ridding of my future. I would throw it in the gutter if it brought you peace. It will never get better if you don't at least try to adapt. You don't want to hear how I am doing. I blocked you out, afraid that I wouldn't be able to obtain inner peace. We hurt each other deeply and deadly. Lost our communication patterns. I'm sorry I don't know how to talk to you anymore. I don't know what to say. Pain brought on by an innocent victim, lost without direction. Where do I go to protect you? Can you protect damaged pieces? Counting down weeks until I see you again. Can you wait? You don't even know me anymore. I don't know me anymore. You did what you thought was best. Now neither of us are getting rest.

RESENTMENT

I don't resent you; you gave me everything. I forgot
where the sacrifice landed. Why do I go on with not
a simple thought going your way? Selfish and greedy,
I'm sorry. I hope you can forgive me too.

NEVER

You were never perfect, but you continued to work for it. Some days were better, others were crippling. I have issues, but I would never push them on you. What do you do when plants die, withered, and dried? Did they fight for their lives the way we fought for ours? I'm much too tired now. Goodbye.

MATTERS

Pure bliss makes mornings like this glorious. Surrounded by what matters most, with the day ahead of me, I can do whatever a heart desires. I don't have to prove who I am. I can just be who I need to be. Others depend on me, and I won't take it lightly. Caring is in my blood. So is my sense of adventure. Let the new day begin.

PLANTED

It was just starting to get fun, making plans to enjoy what time I have remaining. A date has been set, Coming to an end. youth is aging, We need plans to cover ourselves and backup plans for when/if it falls through. Scrapbooks are finished, and photos are tiny glimpses. The time has come. The time is now. I must step forward and collect the reward. This is where I begin, my life in my hands. Adulthood scars worse than a childhood. Nervous hands and shallow breaths. They all watch now as I walk out of those doors for the last time. I was just getting started. Feet were just planted, ready to run. Haven't had time to digest this knowledge. Have I retained the necessary information? Here's to growing up, to new journeys. Here's to pushing on.

PILLS

I lost myself at the bottom of the bottle. I couldn't recognize the person in front of me. When I died, I killed all I was supposed to be. Night terrors told me what would be. Therapists told me what they could see. Cars brought death to me; lack of compassion burned me. I will never be the same. September 18 follows me. I shred memories apart with razor blades. I can't stand to see terrified faces. I am the overcomer. I am the warrior.

BOTTOM

I don't understand. Why would you destroy something so wonderful to explore harmful matter? A selfishness so deep it craters into the very bones of the oppressor. You have gone out of your way to crack the fragile glass protecting the diamond. Undeserving of their valuable attention, you belong among the pebbles lodged in the cracks of the bottom of my shoe.

DESPERATE

Children desperate for love, parents attached to bottles
of many kinds, children longing for affection, parents
undeserving of the title, social workers assisting littles with
their belongings. Tear-filled nights for both sides. Children
wanting Mommy and Daddy. Workers pleading with foster
parents. Adoptions are blessed. Good parents are blessings.

CLUMPED

What do you do when the paint runs out, when the canvas is filled, when you can't find the frame you need? Nothing else will work; it has to be that exact frame. You understand the concept but not what I write, Will I ever find what I need to set this acrylic apart, not like the others, perfectly entwined with the surface underneath? It's worthy of much more. If left in the back, it will surely age without purpose. I must find it. I left it leaning against the wall that traps me. Surrounding me, once again I'm held captive by your everything. Frames weren't meant to bear this much weight. Should've matted, but I never wanted it, to be, like this, to read like this. Eyes shift. What do you do when the paint chips and the fumes go straight to your head? What do I do when I can't find you?

CHIMES

I'm happier now. I found myself dancing to the music in my head, singing to the rhythm of the wind, whistling along to the produce of the chimes. I'm okay, drifting weightlessly.

SEA

You asked me to write about you. Little do you know. Go back
and reread. Every line has been about who I thought I loved, the
one who came and gone, the one who roams my head. You are
"One More" and "Safe Place." You are the pages in between,
the air I breathe, the air I lack. You are the best ones and the
hardest to write, the tears cried, and the, "I'm not over you
yets." The moving on and falling back, the stories I designed.
You will forever be my favorite memory. Somewhere at sea, this
one is for you, the one who stamped themselves on my youth.

It's for you, bright eyes. I wonder if this is your low tide.

BLESSING

The joy that I receive when I see you unexpectedly, seeing you be you. You bring helium to my chest, light and airy. You don't know that I'm here just yet, but that's all right. I watch from the side. When I count my blessings, I count you twice.

STRESS

When the sun comes out, where does the moon go? I know it never leaves. but is it forced to live in the background of the sun, knowing it will never be bright enough to compete with that type of beauty" Overwhelmed and underappreciated, all it wants is to be admired by the one who lights the day. And all the light wants is to be in the background without the stress of pleasing the world. Too much pressure.

FRESH

I'm thankful that He set me free. I wondered how it can be the God of all loves me endlessly, providing me with opportunities and possibilities to speak my mind. Others are silenced for believing. I will not rest. Everyone will know of Your grace and perfect love, Father. Only You can heal broken hearts. You share Your mercy with the lost, the found, and everyone in between. Not to push but to share of the fresh life He provides. Blessed by the One who died and was raised for me. If nothing else sticks, hear Him through me, I love You.

BLISTERS

It's disturbing when someone you cherished runs over each
of your toes, one at a time, blistering every one, knowing
it would hurt. Not supplying because they want to see
the damage. They play the part. Everyone sees the public
treatment. Who really knows what gets whispered?

FRIEND

When I needed you, you laughed. You taught yourself the
way, and you demanded me to do the same. What happened
to our previous ways, when a brother would protect, when
a sister showed respect? Many hands make light work. My
own hands tell me of your selfish ways, all give and no take,
drowning beneath the weight. Filling with water, my lungs
inflate, death brought on by a tidal wave, emotions that will
never know their source. Why are things constantly changing,
evolving into some other form? I do not know the being in
front of me. My eyes seek, searching around you, for I do not
understand what happened to my friend. I cannot recognize the
spirit inside of your shell. Who are you for I do not know?

OCEAN

As the graying clouds pull closer, I seek comfort, the tide that washes away my current, oxygen breathed into me, fish kisses, and lungs from underwater greens. Could this be the deep meaning I'm longing for? Waves closing in on tethered skin, the responsibilities call out my name, but here, here is where I'll be, drawn to the way of the undiscovered. I believe in the life of the tails, powerful and freeing. I'll take my shot and see what drifts along. This could be my sacred place. It's calling me, and I have been renamed.

HANDS

Fresh wants of the heart. With no eyes, it sees what it desires, craves a tender way, the one who started it all. How could one forget enchanted gazes, captivating memories? Brand-new firsts for me. Expectations lost among our pounding hearts, beating that disturbs the flutter in churning stomachs, a fragile beginning. I will remember you. Glad to say I knew you. I memorized the creases in your hands. Without meaning, they whisper, hushed. Some secrets should stay between you and me. You have guided me, gave the setup. I'll take the leap if you will take chances, Wherever I land, you'll be.

ROOTS

The sprout that raised me, weathered my favorite part of history,
I wonder how high you allowed me to climb, tire horses, and
nailed stairs? You were strong during the winters and gave me a
hiding place in other seasons. Leaves that have turned more than
the mill, I thank you for providing such an influential service,
We hung from you and played beside your roots; perhaps that is
why you became a part of me. You were base and our supplier;
our adventure started when we climbed upon you, You held me
from the members and gave me strength, my friend, my tree.

RAGING WAR

I can sense it coming upon us. The humidity bites at my lips.
They swell, blistering to warn of the wrath coming. It will take
me under. The tempestuous skies swarm around me. The buzz
of starving bees ring in my ear. The rage slips through the bars
of caged emotion. The blades from the ground rip and bleed.
The blast of sirens scream in alarm. No one saw it coming.
The shake of various structures reminds us what's at stake. We
will lose it all. The prediction no one could prepare. No one
saw it coming because we all stood before it, eyes closed.

SENTIMENTAL

Everything is of a different shade when little feet challenge the ground. The beating patter sets me in check. Little hearts racing, skin greets the rays from above. The hours before us shine, nudging us to make the best of the day. The sparkle within tiny beings luminate, breaking the bond of a stress-filled day, It is this moment when everything is okay. Tire swings creak and call to our childhood moments. Days like these filled with sweet tea and warm breezes, back porch sitting outside of Grandma's kitchen.

THE AFTERMATH

I'm sorry for when words uttered angered, for when you shoved the joy I had. I must apologize for the years I went out of my way to direct you. The spitting fire in your eye gouged the remains in my throat. The heat your tongue produces. I regret the torment that made you stab at the smile on my cheek. I'm sorry that doused what was left and set it ablaze. You entertain the thoughts you must cast down. The wicked in your heart prevents you from growing. I'm sorry you are you, but I thank God that we're through.

MOTIONS

I can no longer read the story is over. The bitter taste lingers on the buds. I kept the dead flowers; they remain in the glass. I can't seem to let go of what is left. Sorrow is how they describe it, but how do you fix hollow? It's brittle and fragile. It is of an abnormal scent, In need of some sort of charge because I am heartache. I mean heartbroken; I'm not sure what I am at this moment. I believe myself to be wounded, in need of repair. Let me collect dust and then wash me off. But in this moment, please let me be what I be.

108

Could this be? Is the misery coming to an end? Forgotten
how to be natural, normal. I got so used to living like this,
it has become my way. How do you unlearn coping skills?
Can I train myself to act like the others? Will I miss the place
I considered hell? It's all I know. It caused my skin to flake
and gave me rashes, outbreaks. It's my home; it's all I know.
I think I'm ecstatic, I know I'm unsure. Am I really going
to escape, or will it take me, Stockholm Syndrome. I don't
remember how to be clean, not to be in need. Is it time? Am
I being released? Did I do it? Is it a trap? No going back.

SNAPPED

I don't want to talk about the wetness that pours from eyes,
separating myself from my words. So it won't burn, I keep
my headphones in every day. I never lift them from my
ears. They hush the whimpering growl. I blare noise into
my eardrums, so I can't hear them calling my name, They
scratch at my back, leaving keloids and infection. I have
sound screaming at me to protect me. I thought I had found
a way out. I don't fit, My way out of here, I must gnaw at
my remains to lessen my build. I ripped my nails digging
for freedom. One day I'll make it out of here. Until then, I
remain with music cemented to my ears. I will die here.

ELEMENTS

My eyes have fallen. The shape droops, relating to my lips.
Everything sags. The weight of this world has hammered me into
this earth. The rain weathers me, breaking me down, tormenting
the brain in me. Its strings pounding on aging abrasions, I open
cracked lips, hoping to drown. It fills my nose, making me choke.
If I'm choking, I'll survive. I swallow what's left; I accept what
comes. Allowing the reaction, I cough up what was left of my
ignorance. Exposed to the elements, I swallow hard. I swallow
the life I've lived, taking the plunge. Who can hurt me now?

CRIPPLED

The illness came from exposure. I walk among the privileged
to sleep without bugs crawling; to live without mice roaming,
invading rotting floors; feces-wiped walls; and rusted pipes,
A dream it would be to have warm water, food to eat.
Clothes dirtied. The lack of dignity. Cleanliness is hiding
beneath yellow and orange flooring. I want to breathe.
Among pigs, their lifestyle is intentional. Am I leaving soon?
Struggling my whole life through. The air I inhale is polluted
with mold spores. Blackened feet and filthy teeth, the life I
live kills the average. Am I the silent? Am I the needy?

AUGUST 26

A beam that light cannot portray, neighbors with the dimple on your left cheek. It tells of a story, a life you have earned. You held on for so long. This is what you have earned. Battles that you have suffered through. Now is you time. This is the result you were pushing forward for. It will always be a part of you, but now it's no longer your identity. You are finally able to be who you wanted to be. Congratulations, you survived your personalized war. You won't forget the terror, but you bought your future with it. You deserve this happiness. You deserve to smile.

RESET

Thank you, heavenly Father, for showing me what love was.
I have learned from despair and heartache. I have grown in
ways that seem impossible. Every aspect of my life has changed
drastically. I died, and you gave me new life. Everything I
had was ripped away from me. I had to learn how to speak.
I was forced to forgive. I was rewired, and I will never be the
same. I used to think it was punishment, but you stripped
everything to wash me clean. A new life, a new journey, God,
you showed me what it was to live. During the darkest hours,
you held me, the circle and the cycle I was living reset.

ABSENT

I don't go to parties. Not anymore. I can't watch movies at the theater. I drive out of my way to shop at different places. I know I'll run into her, and I'm not ready yet. I can't meet her. They want to know where I am; the life has been absent from these gatherings. I do want to see your face, but I can't, not with her face attached to it. Replaced, I won't allow my eyes to see what I had. I know how much you love the loud music, so I stay home. You should go out, have fun. I just didn't realize she would go with you. This ended, my heart just doesn't know it yet. I continue to miss you. You know where I'll be.

MAGIC

I could go where you lead me. The places I will go—backpacking and exploring, traveling to see the great in this life, the magic each place holds. Cultures, I could learn about other ways. I want to know if the stars look the same there as they do here, all held by the world. How special. Words are different, but the language is the same. Respect the life you live. Live boldly.

WISHED

What is the point of wishes? Who came up with the idea to wish is to have hope for what is next? Aspirations guide the longing for more. I wish for a new state of mind. Wishes fly on the back of the wind. It rises to the ears of angels, allowing the removal of your power, to let go when it's hardest to. The wish travels through many seasons before it can transform into a saving grace, a miracle sent from heaven above. Ask, wish, pray. Never lose the purity that is attached to wishing, stars, wells, fountains, dandelions. Always wish for better, and then be better.

THE TRUTH THAT HIDES

Dreams just don't come true. You work to make them a reality. Patience and perseverance, visions of excellence coming into focus, dreams are more than illusions that come during sleep. They're what calls to you during the storms in your life, destiny waiting for you to welcome it. Dreams don't come true until you find the truth in them. In a world with several lives, choose to live your own. Once you receive your calling, run. Run in the direction that is new to you. Do what is intimidating. Soften your heart, and open your eyes. Use your pain for someone else's benefit, but never hurt yourself for someone's gain. Be the most beautiful version of yourself. Learn to love yourself; appreciate what is around you. We all suffer through something. Don't be quiet. I decided to use my deepest thoughts to paint the picture many don't want to see—confusion, depression, sorrow, anxiety, PTSD. The truth many acknowledge, but not many share, Be open when you're scared. My road is long, however, I know it won't be as dark. I have found a light, and it is because of Him I see, *The Truth That Hides*.